The Worrying Stone

poems by

Benjamin D. Carson

Finishing Line Press
Georgetown, Kentucky

The Worrying Stone

poems by

Benjamin D. Carson

Finishing Line Press
Georgetown, Kentucky

The Worrying Stone

ACKNOWLEDGMENTS

"The Space Between" appeared in *New Plains Review*
"A Late and Final Swim," "What Was Strange, What Familiar," and "The
Wheelbarrow" appeared in *Talking River Review*
"The Hole," "The Trapping Web," "The Final Cut," and "Cedar-Riverside,
Minneapolis, Circa 1990" appeared in *Oakwood*
"Iowa, 1955" appeared in *Waterwheel Review*
"Ascend, Magpie" appeared in *Prometheus Dreaming*
"The Man Who Shot at Birds" appeared in *Unbroken Journal*
"Somewhere Now" appeared in *Mannequin Haus*
"Killing Down the Days" appeared in *South Dakota Magazine*
"Fathers and Sons" appeared in *October Hill Magazine*
"Synchronicity" appeared in *The Chiron Review*
"It is Time" appeared in *Crab Creek Review*
"Requiem in Starbucks" appeared in *Edify Fiction*

Publisher: Leah Huete de Maines
Editor: Christen Kincaid
Cover Art: Scott Lemon
Author Photo: Andrea Kamins
Cover Design: Elizabeth Maines McCleavy

Order online: www.finishinglinepress.com
also available on amazon.com

Author inquiries and mail orders:
Finishing Line Press
PO Box 1626
Georgetown, Kentucky 40324
USA

Contents

for Ted Richer
poet, mentor, friend

The Space Between

(for Diane and Jerry Lagadec)

As a poet, I do not write about seasons,
winter's cutting edge or summers late to leave.
I do not write about love and its complexities, and
I don't, in words, praise the dead or mourn the living.

I do not write about bones that complain like the floors
of an old house, or trees and their windfall, or birds
that circle in hunger, or those paths, overgrown and
narrow, that carry us deeper into the woods.

I do not write about temptation or the pleasures of sin,
the stubbed toe of conscience delayed in its warning.
I do not write of Mont Blanc or the Matterhorn, the
Gardens of Babylon or the Colossus of Rhodes.

It's lighter than that, and heavier. I write
about space, the space between breaths
—where everything comes and where
everything goes.

Cedar-Riverside, Minneapolis, Circa 1990

"Dog-tired, suisired, will now my body down
near Cedar Avenue in Minneap,
where my crime comes."
        "The Poet's Final Instruction," John Berryman

We small-town kids, refugees from the Dakota plains, screamed
our way into one half of this twin city and, each in our turn,
were forged by its streets and seared in the alembic of adolescent
mania. From the 8th floor of a high-rise, flecked with Rothkos—
fading panels of blue and white and red and yellow—and with a
view of the Mississippi and the bridge from which Berryman took
a fatal plunge, we blazed, shorn of sense, muddle-brained,
and found company, our tribe, in the patients on the ward of Cedar
and Riverside: Earthy B and his pyramid of televisions, Shorty Mac
and his Night Train, and Ten Bear trading peyote for pot.

And it was on this corner where Phil, whose preferred poetic form
was fists, failed to match wits, one flailing night, with a one-armed
Ethiopian, who, having unscrewed his hand from his arm, stamped
his prosthetic poetry of war on Phil's deserving face, blue-black
spondees on his cheeks and jowl. Enjambment.

And it was here, in a frenzy of insobriety, the contents of our
refrigerator flew from the balcony as though we, the wardens
of the ward, were feeding sharks from the bow of a listing ship,
the hull vomiting up chum, a blitz of food-bombs raining down
on rooftops, victuals for scavengers in a sea of concrete and noise.
Pin joints, sustenance of a kind, hid under the microwave,
an amuse-bouche.

In the foam and froth of youth, we, indignant spirits unbound,
were hungry, fed by the urge to shape something, to name
the rinds of waste that mottle the cityscape, to give rise to a poem
in which we, the new arrivals, fresh flotsam, washed up as we were
from a sea of grass, got to the heart of something, set the rhythm,
the "I AMs," to an unsettled life; and so it was here, on this corner,

overlooking rooftops and the bridge from which Berryman took
a fatal plunge, that we, for a time, lived, the place
where Cedar meets Riverside.

Ascend, Magpie
(for Kayo)

> *"It was also my violent heart that broke,*
> *Falling down the front hall stairs."*
> —Anne Sexton, *"The Break"*

She was, and I told her she was,
this long-time bride of mine and madness,
non compos mentis, after she hurled
herself, ragdoll, all dressed in nothing,
down that flight of stairs. "A magpie,"
she said, in a raspy chatter, pulling at her hair,
a heap on the floor, shattered. "I ascend,"
she said, pie-eyed, as though too high to be heard,
and I said, yes, ascend, Magpie, and fly, fly again

An Artifact of Loneliness

In an old book,
a strand of her hair.

Iowa, 1955

It was in the old barn, she said, two miles south of Lovett's Crossing,
where her cousin Leroy, that late Sunday afternoon, pushed her down,
put his fingers to her lips and hissed, *this is what God wants.* Swallows
nested in the rafters—will they sing of this?—mice, like her fists,
burrowed in the hay. Somewhere, far off, a train whistle blew,
and the odor of sweetgrass mingled with blood and snot. It was
the moment my grandmother knew she'd leave this place, not just this
old barn, two miles south of Lovett's Crossing, but this land they call
Iowa. She'd find the ocean, live in its depths. I'll rest at the bottom,
she told herself, as the dust kicked up around her, and, in the absence
of words, learn the language of water, one inhalation at a time.

Killing Down the Days

I was twelve when I pulled the trigger
and made that porcupine dead. The old
farmer said shoot it, its back up and round
like a tumble weed, its bristles golden in the
morning sun, nothing at all like a deer. I don't
know why I did what he said, the old farmer,
whom I was too young to know and just young
enough to obey, his prickly beard and pulled
down hat lost to me now. I dragged the animal
from its burrow, its legs as thick as my wrists,
a prize to show my brothers, a trophy for my
father. My brothers oohed and felt its weight
with their boots; my father said get in the truck,
and, just like that, we left it to the wolves and
the worms. And thirty-five years on, I can still
see, as we rolled out of that pasture, my kill, a
spent shell, nothing now but a lumpen memory,
like a mound of flesh living in the throat, that on
the coldest nights, alone, I wonder about, but
I still can't close the distance.

The Man Who Shot at Birds

I heard it told of a man who shot at birds, his porch wrecked
with shells spit from his gun. His hooked nose and gimlet
eyes flush against the stock, he aimed for their wings, their
beaks, and he aimed for their eyes. He liked to watch them
flail, he said, a ballet of feathers, as they fell, notes on an
atonal, descending scale. He said he liked to hear a clipped
song sung by a nicked tongue, while they flew and flew and
flew, blind. Wounded, he'd say, is just as good as dead. And I
heard it told that when he died, his body still warm, his arms
splayed like plucked wings, a chorus erupted, a dirge, and the
trees pulsed with a murder of crows.

Fathers and Sons

(for Kenneth Rexroth)

In the summer of nineteen nighty-nine
I read Turgenev's *Fathers and Sons*.
That fall my father had a stroke, and
in the spring, he died. In the hours
before he took his last breath, I went
in search of a poem on dying by Yeats.
I never did find it. It may not even exist.
I returned to my father's bedside in time
for the death rattle, dying's own kind of
poem, I guess; and then he went his way,
and I went mine.

Last night I had a dream; my father was
drunk, unshaven, and trying to hit me.
All of my dreams about him are like this:
a kind and gentle, habitually sober man in
life, in my sleep is always angry, and I the
object of his wrath. He tells me I am not
serious, that I am a fool. He pushes me,
his undershirt wet with sweat, and his hair
a mop of rage. In these dreams I hate my
father, a man I know now I never really
knew, a man I never hated but am not
sure I ever loved.

This morning my son told me he'd had
a dream: I was chasing him through a field
of wheat. He could feel me fast on his heels,
my breath on his neck, and he, for a moment,
thought I was laughing, but when I caught him,
he said my eyes were filled with liquid. He said
he pushed the hair away from my eyes and saw
his own reflection—a boy, as small as a bird, held
firmly in two large hands against a backdrop of land
and sky, and he knew that I loved him, and that he
was safe, though he knew not from what or for how
long.

Requiem in Starbucks

Requiem aeternam dona eis, Domine
—*Prayer from the Liturgy of the Hours*

I saw a couple getting divorced today,
or rather the sordid penultimate powwow
before the judge's gavel declares this play
dead. They must have been married sixty-
years, the way they went at each other's
throats, clawing at whatever thing they
could get to better bleed out the one
person for whom, years ago, they'd for-
sworn all others. "I get the lamp, John,"
she said. "It was my grandmother's, and
only I ever read under it. Books, John.
You know what books are?" This John,
who, over the lip of his coffee cup, had
the eyes of a man drowning, whispered,
"I'm in the Math department, Martha.
The Math department." I could see she
didn't want to take the bait but she was
determined, and I, who only came to read
—books, John, you know what those are?
—was now in their slipstream, their wake.
"My name is not Martha, John, and you are
not in the Math department. I get the lamp,
and you, you can have the rest." "*A* rest,
Martha." John said. "*A* rest. I can have *a* rest,
now that *you* are gone."

Martha. My grandmother's name. She
kicked my grandfather out with nothing
but his belt buckle and an old pair of boots,
said nothing he ever did added up, nothing
he ever said rang true, aligned with anything
she ever knew. Martha, my mother's name,
slipped off without a sound as I took the stage
some forty odd years ago. My father, for all

the world, might as well be a "John," a man
whom I never knew nor whose name I ever heard.

So many leavings, I thought to myself as I got
up to go, unwilling to watch these two tally up
and haggle over bits of jetsam flung from the bow
of their sinking union, their final act. Over my
shoulder I heard, "my name . . . is *not* . . . Martha,"
but I had to wonder.

What Was Strange, What Familiar

From my elevated bed I can see out the window
to the cemetery, and the late afternoon light and
the early spring breeze, for a moment, render my
room unfamiliar. It's Urbana-Champaign, I think,
wherever that is, and rest there for a moment, taking
it in. It feels good to be somewhere else, somewhere
new, just for a time, knowing I am not really there at all.
From my bed I can see a gravedigger leaning against
his shovel, smoking a cigarette, and I can feel my lungs
expand, take in the smoke, exhale, as the air grows heavy,
the light grows dim, and what was then strange and what
is now familiar fades to black.

And in the Silence the Poet Wonders

(for Ted Richer)

When the cancer
in his lungs
made its way
to his throat
and the Poet
lost his voice,
he found he
couldn't write.
And in the
silence, he wondered
what, if anything,
he had left
to say was
even worth saying.
And so, in
the silence, he
wondered, wonders still.

Carved in Stone

It's been a year since I bought my gravestone,
and I'm still alive. I had "Here Lies the Body of an
Old Man" inscribed on it, thinking that, as long as
I wasn't old, it had nothing to do with me. For now,
I just have to live, to breathe in the days' promises,
none of which are carved in stone.

The Wheelbarrow

Behind the old barn a wheelbarrow casts a shadow
—over cans of paint and oil, a carburetor, the rear
door of an Edsel—its body now bearded by rust,
its handles raised in surrender, flush against a shed,
its lone tire disfigured by the memory of a child pushed
by his sister, a litter of kittens, kindling for a fire, what
was left of my grandfather after tangling with an auger,
bales of hay the only witness to his undoing. Empty now
but not unburdened, forgotten but unable to forget, it holds
itself up, having done its time, having pulled its weight.

A Late and Final Swim

(for SS)

She said she wasn't drowning but waving
when I pulled her from the lake, though she
thought, at times, she said, of sinking beneath
the waves, of breathing in the water, a late and
final swim, going down.

*I bet you thought you were some kind of
hero,* she said, *lifting me up from the dead,
Lazarus-like, some kind of savior.*

No, I said. *Maybe,* I said, and walked away.
Waving. Drowning.

The Final Cut

I cut up a poem, I confess, and want to keep what is left,
consonants and vowels like fingers and toes
scattered on a highway. And I wonder:
what if we didn't murder to dissect
but to murd and er and diss and ect,
left parts un-scrutinized, only sounds of a crime:
a gurgle, a slashing of sorts, in the throat.

I move my fingers across a scar on my lover's wrist,
and over the ridges on her thighs, tracks to nowhere,
and say nothing, just worry them, lines indelible.
Then, just above a whisper, she says, I dreamt of birds,
a wake of vultures, picking at my flesh, and I await, await now
the final cut.

Memories Future Past

I shall never know why
Our lives took a turn for the worse, nor will you.
            —*Mark Strand*

I will one day remember things we have not yet done,
a future past, and I will frame those moments, carve them
out against a backdrop of good intentions gone bad,
bad nights that bled into gray mornings, and weeks and
months of solitude beside her. I'll remember her saying,
"this is not how it has to be." And I'll remember me wondering
how exactly it is or how it got this way. She will tell me I have
amnesia, that I have forgotten who we are, who we were,
and I'm thinking now that I will one day deny it, say I know,
that I remember, even though I don't. And one day I'll
remember that I was supposed to recall these things,
but I know now, in the present, that, in the future,
I will neither remember nor care.

Synchronicity

I couldn't tell you the last time I felt tethered to something,
experienced one of those moments when the universe fools me
into thinking coincidences are brush strokes on the tableau that,
upon my death, would be my life: like the time I stepped off the
F train with a tattered copy of *Bury My Heart at Wounded Knee*
to find a Buffalo Nickel; or the time the friend I dreamt about
called in the morning just to say she was dying—moments
of improbable synchronicity that pull together the filaments
in the fabric of my private cosmos, my personal singularity.
Maybe these moments really are fool's gold, rare as they are,
errant errands into a tangled wilderness, knots, rather than
signposts or cairns on an un-folding mindscape. Maybe.
But they just might be enough, enough to keep me from being
thrown off this bucking planet and into the ether.

It is Time

It was last month or maybe last week, she said,
when the floor gave way beneath her feet.
Her life, she told me, was like an old house,
gables of mold and rot, windows cracked,
unmoored from their panes, rattling with
the wind, the foundation listing, built, as it was,
on sand or, given the smell, a landfill.
It is time, she said. It is time for a fire.

The Hole

She stood looking into the darkness,
as if waiting for it to speak, to reveal
something about itself. This was the
first time she'd seen the hole, the hole
behind her house and the nothingness
it cradled. She didn't know where it'd
come from or who'd dug it. When she
knelt close to its open mouth, cool air
breathed her hair back, and she closed
her eyes to listen. She felt a stone beneath
her hand, rubbed it between her fingers,
and then brought it to her lips. "Gone,"
she whispered, before dropping it into
the hole. She waited, ear to its lip, and
waited, hearing only silence in reply.

The Trapping Web

All of that is nothing to me, she says, reaching
toward the sky, as if the gesture would free her from
the bullseye. I will not look back, she says, craning
her neck, the sting of salt in her eyes.

I'm out, she says, laughing, as if that too will
leave her unencumbered, free of night sweats,
the shadows that move in her room after sundown,
saying, we are still here.

It's nothing, she shrugs, as the spider circles,
spinning its trapping web around her legs and arms,
her mouth. And she thinks: How lucky it is to unspool itself
in thin pearls of only now, now, and now.

The Worrying Stone

The sun was low on the horizon and
the tide was out when I went looking
for a poem. There were beach stones,
one gray with white rivulets like rivers
on the moon that I worried as I walked
the sand into the fading light. A salt-soaked
gull swung low, swept back and down,
hopped along, dappled, dancing in the grating
roar, waves like thunder and foam, and, further out,
a seal rolled, a shadow now in the fog of
dusk. I walked until the moon rose, worrying
that stone, reading its lines with my thumb,
feeling rhythm, the beat of words beyond
words, the rough poetry of things.

As I Ran on the Beach, a Seagull

As I ran on the beach, a seagull,
maybe a cormorant,
flew up beside me,
and I ran and it flew,
and just for a moment,
to the applause of the lapping waves,
we raced to the West,
to the place where the light fades
and everything sleeps.

Somewhere Now

Somewhere, maybe near you, a man is drinking himself to death, and somewhere a man is shitting in a hole. Somewhere a woman is hailing a cab, and another is ordering a Merlot. Somewhere a man is duct taping his girlfriend's hands and tickling her nipples with a feather, and just north of Schenectady, in a place called Scotia, a man is burying a cat. His sister is looking for her keys. At this moment, somewhere, a woman is waiting and wanting to die, and somewhere a child is foaming at the mouth in the backseat of a hot car, her mother shopping for a birthday card. In India a man waits for a train and a woman bathes in the Ganges. A man eats sushi in Japan, another eats sushi in Miami, and somewhere a girl named Porsche is braiding her hair. Someone somewhere is chewing gum, and somewhere a teenager is driving his car into the side of a van driven by a woman. Someone somewhere is wondering about the woman he killed. Somewhere a trucker looks to pick up a hitchhiker, and somewhere a hitchhiker waits for a ride. A boy is meeting now with a girl who, in a year, he will ask to be his wife. They are young but so is the boy eating out of the garbage in Tuscaloosa. A woman, six months pregnant, falls down the stairs and is bleeding into her underwear. A woman caught in traffic curses her luck. Somewhere in Cambodia a man vomits in an alley, and someone somewhere is being diagnosed with cancer and someone is being robbed and someone is putting a cotton swab in his ear and someone is playing the violin. Right now, a guy is filling his car with gas and wondering how far he'll make it before he's far enough away to forget her. A farmer is praying for rain. A boy is wondering if it's wrong to be aroused by his cousin who is a boy who, like him, loves Jesus. A grandmother is winning at Rummy and a granddaughter is riding her bike into the street. A mailman is running over a child who rode her bike into the street. This is happening. It's happening now: a boy touching himself for the first time, a girl taking a sip of her father's beer, a father dropping a hammer on his toe, a brother choking on a bone. A dog is getting lost and a chicken is getting its throat cut. A child who fell off of a moving train is being run over, the toes of his bodiless leg are twitching and ants smell the blood. A woman inhales smoke from the fire that will kill her, and someone smashes a tv set at a motel in Laramie. Girls are on their phones and boys are on their phones. College students are drinking coffee and questioning everything. Someone somewhere is confessing. A woman is writing a novel and wondering where the story's going. A grandfather is wondering where the time went. Somewhere a man is whipping a box with a belt and someone is making a sign for a protest. Right now, somewhere, people are against things. A man in Budapest is leaning against a lamp post and humming "Himnusz." Somewhere an athlete is kneeling. A bird is dying. A squirrel is building a nest. A rat is eating a body in an elevator shaft in Detroit. A boat is sinking. An uncle is drowning. A sister is cursing. A man named Daryl is in prison and passing a kite. Somewhere a woman is saying "enough," and a man is turning off a radio. A police officer is arrested for being drunk and disorderly in a bar on the edge of Milwaukee. A man with a limp is limping. Somewhere a man with a limp is grateful. A woman is faking an orgasm. A boy is smelling his finger. Someone is writing a poem. Somewhere a man sharpens a blade, another polishes a boot. A man is led through the streets by a rope, a mother crosses a border, a child dies in a desert. Someone smoking is watching someone dying and is laughing. A boy plays the harmonica, another catches a fish. A French Traveler wonders what he'll play tonight at Barbès in Brooklyn. A couple kisses in Central Park and two men enjoy hamburgers in Redwater. There is an alligator digesting a dog and a man is loading a gun. A woman is praying in Rome, a man is praying in Paris, parishioners are praying in Mt. Willing. Somewhere right now, maybe near you, a child is being born.

With Thanks

For their encouragement, inspiration, support, and friendship, I'd like to thank:

Rob Radack, Lillian LaSalle, Kelly Clough Brown, George Heck, Jenni Zickert, Casey and Lana Gooby, Tonya Moutray, Lori LeComte, Joshua Doležal, Gervase Hittle, Andrea Julie Kamins, Bernie Hunhoff, Katie Hunhoff, John Andrews, Dee Carson (mom), and Robert, Kellie, and Sarah Carson.

Thank you to all the literary magazine and journal editors, especially Leah Huete de Maines and Christen Kincaid, who took a chance on my work.

Thank you, Scott, for the beautiful cover photo. Thank you, Andrea, for the mug shot.

I would like to express my gratitude to the men, my brothers, at Old Colony Correctional Center—may the light in me honor the light in you.

A special thank you to Clarence Major, Diane Glancy, and Steven Wingate.

This book is dedicated to Ted Richer, a poet, a mentor, and a friend. May he rest in peace.

Benjamin D. Carson is a Professor of English at Bridgewater State University. His creative work appears or is forthcoming in many literary journals, including *Rumble Fish Quarterly, Yellow Medicine Review, Cactus Heart,* and *South Dakota Review.* He is the author of *We Give Birth to Light: Poems* (Finishing Line Press, 2021).